W is for Waves

An Ocean Alphabet

Written by Marie and Roland Smith and Illustrated by John Megahan

A special thanks to Joan McClelland for introducing us to her husband, Scott, whose knowledge of the oceans was so helpful.

—Marie and Roland Smith

Sleeping Bear Press™

310 North Main Street, Suite 300
Chelsea, MI 48118
www.sleepingbearpress.com

© 2008 Sleeping Bear Press is an imprint of Gale, a part of Cengage Learning.

Printed and bound in the United States.

10 9 8 7 6 5 4 3 2 1

Library of Congress Cataloging-in-Publication Data

Smith, Marie, 1951-
W is for waves : an ocean alphabet / written by Marie and Roland Smith
; illustrated by John Megahan. — 1st ed.
p. cm.
Summary: "An A to Z introduction to our world's oceans and ocean life.
Topics include Atlantis, kelp forests, the Great Barrier Reef, mollusks,
Queen Isabella, and many more"—Provided by publisher.
ISBN 978-1-58536-254-7
1. Ocean—Juvenile literature. 2. Marine biology—Juvenile literature.
3. English language—Alphabet—Juvenile literature. I. Smith, Roland, 1951-
II. Megahan, John. III. Title.
GC21.5.S635 2008
551.46—dc22   2007034586

For Mom and Dad—the best Shipmates we could ever ask for.

Love,

MARIE & ROLAND

〜

To Mom and Dad, and also to all my helpers,
Nicholas, Ian, Emily, Benjamin, Daniel, Rivka, and especially Anne.

With Love,

JOHN

Plato, an ancient Greek philosopher and teacher, wrote about an island called Atlantis. Atlantis belonged to Poseidon, the god of the sea from Greek mythology. According to Plato, Poseidon built his wife, Cleito, a home in the very middle of Atlantis. Atlas, their oldest son, became the king. For generations the Atlanteans lived a peaceful and prosperous life. Then Atlantis and all of its people disappeared beneath the sea—destroyed by the gods who felt they had become corrupted by power and greed. Some historians believe Atlantis is somewhere in the middle of the Atlantic Ocean; some say it is in the Mediterranean Sea. Others believe it is on the island of Santorini where a volcanic eruption covered it in ash. Thousands of stories and books have been written about Atlantis. People have spent lifetimes trying to find this mythical island, but so far no one ever has.

The mystery of Atlantis is thousands of years old but our oceans hold mysteries that are even older. This book is about some of the things we do know about our oceans.

A is for Atlantis—
gone forever more.
Scientists still searching
along the ocean floor.

Beaches are the sloping shores next to the ocean that are constantly changed by the washing of the tides and waves. Perhaps the beach near you is sandy, a perfect place to build sand castles. Other beaches are covered with rocks that rockhounds, people who collect rocks, like to visit. Sand comes in many colors from almost white to black. It can be made from rocks like quartz or coral shells that have decomposed. Waves and tides coming in grind rocks and shells into different sizes and shapes until they are turned into sand. Scientists classify rocks by their size. Rocks the size of basketballs are called boulders. Rocks the size of grapefruit are called cobbles and rocks the size of golf balls are called pebbles.

Many people walk along the beach after a storm or when the tide goes out to beachcomb, searching for keepsakes left on the beach. If you visit the beach on the east coast of the United States you may wake up to see a fiery sunrise; if you visit the beach on the west coast you may enjoy a glowing sunset before it's time for bed.

B is for Beaches.
Build a castle in a day.
Oops—watch out for waves
they'll wash it all away.

Many sea creatures use camouflage. Camouflage means to disguise or conceal. When an octopus senses danger it protects itself by changing the pattern or color of its skin to match its environment. The decorator crab dresses itself to look like its surroundings by using objects it finds on the ocean floor. Scorpion fish resemble the coral reefs or the rocky bottoms where they live. Nearly invisible, it waits for some tasty unsuspecting fish and gulps it down.

C is also for current. A current is the flow of water from one place to another. Ocean currents form mostly due to the actions of the wind and the sun on the Earth. Winds move back and forth across the oceans pushing surface waters. When the surface waters reach the western shores they go north or south to the poles. Once it reaches the poles the water is cooled and falls toward the bottom and is replaced by the water heated at the equator causing large circular currents in the ocean.

Currents also form when the sun evaporates ocean water. The salt is left behind making the remaining water heavier. The heavier water sinks to the bottom pushing up the lighter, less salty water, creating motion called *thermohaline* (therm-oh-HAY-leen) currents or density currents.

C is for Camouflage.
Sea creatures use this trick
against animals that eat them
or to eat the ones they pick!

D is for Dolphins—
jumping along
in front of ships
singing a song.

Dolphins are intelligent, friendly, have a natural sense of curiosity, and use different sounds to communicate. For no apparent reason they seem to enjoy hanging out where people are. Dolphins, porpoises, and whales are *cetaceans* (si-TAY-shuns) from the Latin word *cetus*, meaning "a large sea creature." Dolphins, porpoises, and whales are mammals like us. They are warm blooded, give birth to live young, nurse their young, and breathe air through lungs. They have adapted to living in the water with extra body fat called blubber and have bodies that are streamlined to swim fast.

Despite its name, the killer whale is actually a dolphin, not a whale. It is called a whale because of its great size. Sometimes they can be over 32 feet long and weigh over 18,000 pounds. They are also known as orcas. Other marine mammals include seals, sea lions, walruses, sea otters, dugongs, manatees, and polar bears.

Dd

Prince William Sound is in Alaska. A sound is a wide inlet of the sea or ocean that is parallel to the coastline. In 1989 the supertanker, *Exxon Valdez*, carrying crude oil struck Bligh Reef. The hull of the ship ruptured and over 11 million gallons of oil spilled into the water. Seabirds, sea otters, seals, whales, and many other animals and plants were killed by this oil spill. It was the largest oil spill in the U.S. After this oil spill, congress passed the Oil Pollution Act of 1990, which required the Coast Guard to strengthen its regulations on oil tank vessels, oil tank owners, and operators. The largest oil spill in the world happened in the Persian Gulf when more than 250 million gallons of oil soaked into the coastline of Saudi Arabia.

E is also for *echinoderms* (ee-KI-noh-derms) or spiny-skin. Echinoderms have five-fold symmetry meaning they have arms or rays in multiples of five. Sea stars, sea lilies, brittle stars, sea urchins, and sea cucumbers are all echinoderms.

E is for the *Exxon Valdez*—
a ship that ran aground,
spilling 11 million gallons of oil
into Prince William Sound.

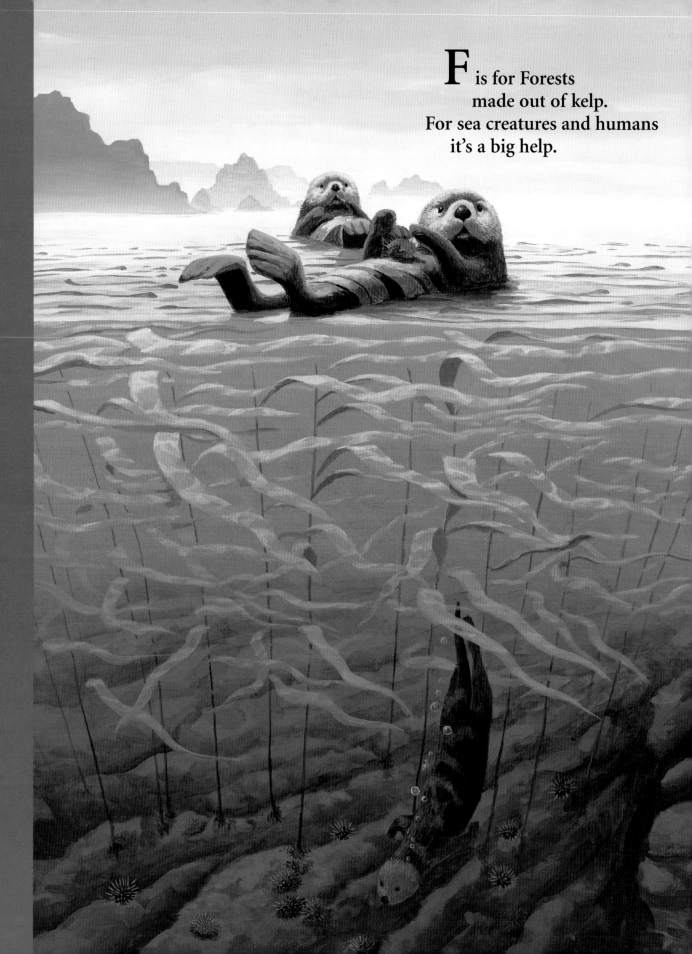

Ff

F is for Forests
made out of kelp.
For sea creatures and humans
it's a big help.

Kelp is a form of algae. Algae are plants that grow in seawater or freshwater. The ones that grow in the ocean are often called seaweed. Large numbers of kelp growing together can form an underwater forest that becomes home for many sea creatures like the sea otter. Sometimes sea otters nap wrapped up in a long blade of kelp using it as an anchor. It keeps them from floating too far out in the ocean. Kelp is an important food source for sea creatures and for people around the world. It is used to make medicines, vitamins, cosmetics, salad dressings, and even ice cream. Gardeners use it as fertilizer to help plants grow. Kelp forests provide a buffer or barrier to protect shorelines from strong waves during a storm.

F is also for fish. The oceans are full of them. Scientists have identified more than 20,000 kinds of fish and are finding more all the time. You know it is a fish if it has a backbone and gills.

The Great Barrier Reef—
thousands travel to see
this unique underwater park
that starts with the letter G.

More than two million people visit the Great Barrier Reef of Australia each year. It contains the world's largest collection of coral reefs; it's not one reef but more than 3,000 reefs covering 1,200 miles in the Coral Sea. It is even visible from the moon. The coral reef is made up of thousands and thousands of tiny sea creatures called polyps living in groups called colonies. They produce a shell to live in with the help of a tiny plant that grows inside them. They are constantly adding on to their homes, one layer on top of the other. The reef has around 400 types of coral, 800 species of echinoderms, 500 species of seaweed, 1,500 species of fish, 1,500 species of sponge, 4,000 types of *mollusk* (MOL-uhsk) and more than 30 species of marine mammals including the dugong. Don't forget reptiles! The large green sea turtle, which is threatened with extinction, also makes the Great Barrier Reef its home.

G is also for the Gulf Stream, a strong ocean current in the Atlantic Ocean. It's like a river inside the ocean that flows along the eastern coast of the United States, past Nova Scotia then over to Europe. Benjamin Franklin and his cousin, Timothy Folger, a whaling ship captain, drew the first chart of the Gulf Stream in 1769. There is a similar northern current near Japan called the Kuroshio Current.

Gg

H h

H is for Horses,
these are so small,
they live in the ocean
not ridden at all!

Remember Poseidon from Atlantis? He used a giant sea horse to pull his chariot through the ocean. Sea horses are fish. They are cousins to sea dragons, pipefish, and pipehorses. They belong to a family called *syngnathidae* (sing-nath-i-dee). They have tube-shaped snouts with small mouths. Males in this group of fish have a special pouch to protect and nurture the eggs given to them from the female. The male takes care of the eggs until they hatch. Approximately 35 seahorse species have been identified. Seahorses live along coastlines hiding among beds of sea grass, mangrove roots, and coral reefs.

H is also for *humuhumunukunukuapua'a*! (HOO-moo-HOO-moo-NOO-koo-NOO-koo-AH-poo-AH-ah). It is a fish found in the Hawaiian Islands and other Pacific Ocean locations. It means trigger fish with a blunt snout like a pig. It makes a squeaking noise like a pig too. It is the state fish of Hawaii.

Icebergs are chunks of ice that have broken off a freshwater glacier, ice sheet, or ice shelf; when this happens it is called calving. Because icebergs are made of freshwater they are not as dense as the salt water they float in. Only one-seventh to one-tenth of an iceberg's mass shows above water. Most of their mass is hidden underneath the water making them very dangerous for ships or boats.

I is also for island. Greenland is the largest island in the world. Eighty percent of Greenland is covered with ice. Most of the icebergs floating in the Northern Hemisphere come from Greenland. It is home to the largest land predator—the polar bear. These beautiful white bears can stand 10 feet tall and weigh up to 2,000 pounds. They are not afraid of anything! They depend on the ocean for their food supply and seals are a favorite meal.

Another I word is *invertebrate* (in-VUR-tuh-brit)—any animal that does not have a backbone. Some invertebrates are sea jelly, octopus, squid, crab, lobster, shrimp, sea *anemone* (uh-NEM-uh-nee), sponge, corals, clams, oysters, barnacles, scallops, sea urchins, and sea cucumbers.

I i

I is for Iceberg.
Harmless looking as they float
but what lies beneath the water
may destroy your boat.

J j

J is for Jacques Cousteau.
He helped us to know
all about the oceans
aboard his ship *Calypso*.

Jacques Cousteau was a pioneer in underwater photography. He was born in France and became interested in photography at a young age. In 1943, he and Emile Gagnan, a French engineer, invented the Self-Contained Underwater Breathing Apparatus known as SCUBA. This gave freedom to divers wanting to explore the oceans. Many people remember him most for his TV series *The Undersea World of Jacques Cousteau* filmed aboard his ship the *Calypso*.

Another pioneer in ocean exploration was Marie Tharp. She was a cartographer, a person that draws maps. She charted the bottom of the ocean during the 1940s and 50s when very little was known about the ocean floor.

Rachel Carson was a pioneer in writing about the ocean. She wrote best selling books including *The Sea Around Us*, *The Edge of the Sea* and *Silent Spring*. Her writing inspired people all over the world to change the way they think about their relationship with the environment.

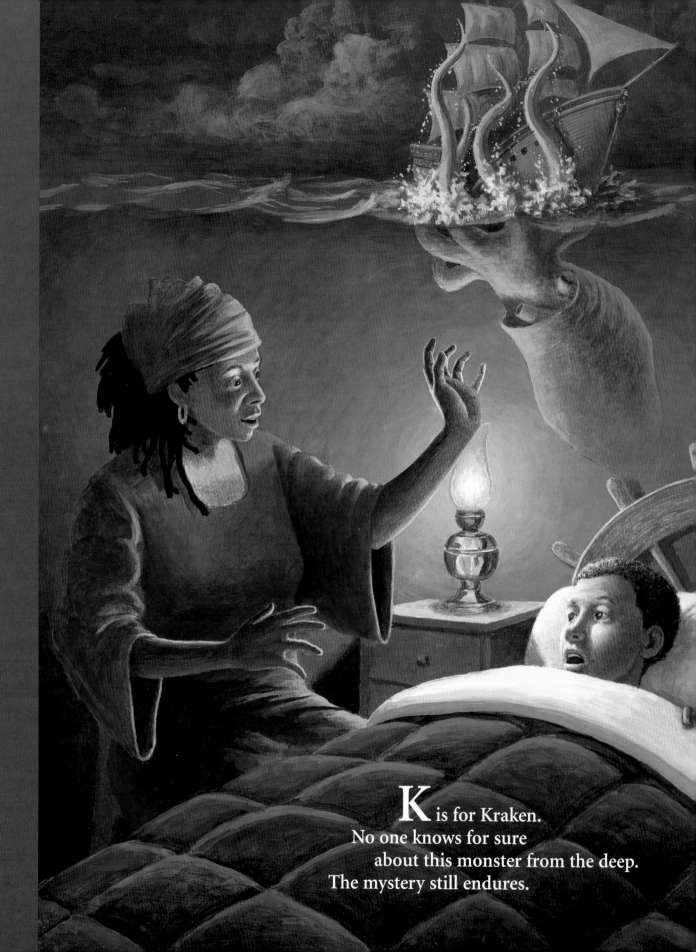

Centuries ago sailors told stories about the Kraken, a huge sea monster big as an island that lived off the coast of Norway and Sweden. Sailors said it could wrap its arms around a ship and bring it down to the ocean floor. The giant squid might have been the inspiration for this story. Giant squid or *Architeuthis dux* (ark-ee-TOO-this do) are thought to be over 60 feet long and have eyes about 15 inches in diameter. That makes them the largest of all invertebrates with the largest eyes in the Animal Kingdom. The giant squid is still a mystery since only a few have ever been seen alive. We still don't know how big they can get, how they live, or what they normally eat.

The name Kraken is from a Norwegian word meaning uprooted tree. When big trees are uprooted along the shoreline they sometimes float upside down in the ocean with their roots sticking above the surface. If seen late at night this may look like "hands" or "arms" reaching toward a ship. Only when the sun comes up do sailors realize a tree was chasing them! This may be another source of the Kraken stories.

K is for Kraken.
No one knows for sure
about this monster from the deep.
The mystery still endures.

Bioluminescence is the generation of light by living organisms. About 90% of deep sea fish use *bioluminescence* (bahy-oh-loo-muh-NES-uhns). Some use it to attract a mate; some use it to camouflage themselves against the light that filters from above; and others like the flashlight fish, use it to find food or to communicate with each other. The flashlight fish has eyelids that allow it to turn on and off its lights. Some anglerfish have a lure-like body part that lights up and dangles in front of their mouth, enticing victims in for dinner. Some star- fish, sea cucumbers, and shrimp also use bioluminescence.

L is also for laws. The Law of the Sea Treaty is an agreement between countries that protects territorial waters and governs ocean dumping, fishing, endangered species, sea-lanes, and ocean resources. Countries around the world have signed this treaty. The U.S. has signed this agreement but the senate has not ratified it.

L l

L is for Lights,
some sea creatures have their own.
Great to have if the lights go out
at night when you're all alone.

M is for Mollusks. This popular group often end up in somebody's soup.

Have you ever enjoyed a hot steaming bowl of clam chowder? If you have, you were eating just one of the 100,000 species of animals called mollusks. Mollusks are soft-bodied animals. Most mollusks have a shell on the outside but some have them on the inside. For centuries people have considered the shells from mollusks as treasures, using them for jewelry, art, even money. Oysters are mollusks and give us one of the most coveted ocean treasures of all—the pearl. A person who studies and collects shells is called a conchologist.

M is also for Mariana Trench found in the Pacific Ocean. It is the deepest part of the ocean. The deepest part of the Trench is known as the Challenger Deep. The Challenger Deep is 35,800 feet below sea level—that is almost 7 miles!

One more **M**—migration: the regular travel from one place to another. Many sea creatures migrate. Every fall large groups of spiny lobster line up single file, each in contact with the one in front and migrate for deeper water where it is warmer during the winter. Baby salmon, called *alevin* (al-uh-vuhn), hatch in freshwater then swim downstream to the ocean where they spend up to four years before migrating back to the same rivers they came from.

M
m

N is for the North Star.
Sailors used it to navigate
before the compass or sextant,
keeping their course straight.

Getting lost at sea was a problem for early sailors who had none of the instruments that make travel so easy today. The North Star, also called Polaris, is part of the constellation Ursa Minor. Early sailors like the Phoenicians used this special star for navigation. It is above the North Pole and marks due north.

The compass and sextant were also valuable navigational tools for sailors to use. But sailors still had trouble, so in 1714 the British government offered a cash prize for anyone who could solve the problem of finding longitude.

In 1764, John Harrison invented the chronometer and eventually won the prize. The chronometer is a clock that keeps accurate time while at sea. It was used to figure out distance between two locations. Explorer James Cook used the very first marine chronometer to chart parts of the Pacific Ocean's coastline including the islands of New Zealand and Tahiti. The wristwatch is a result of the invention of the chronometer.

Ocean comes from the Greek word *okeanos* meaning river. The planet Earth could have been called the "planet ocean," since oceans cover more than 70% of the Earth's surface. All the oceans are connected. Seas, bays, and gulfs are bodies of water that branch off oceans and are partially enclosed by land. We have five distinct oceans. The Pacific is the largest; the Atlantic is the second largest and busiest for ship travel; the Indian Ocean is the third largest; the smallest is the Arctic Ocean and in 2000, the Southern Ocean became our newest. The oceans are the most populated places on Earth —filled with billions of fish, mammals, reptiles, invertebrates, and plants. The ocean is important to all of our lives on a daily basis. It provides nourishment for our bodies, rain for our produce, and transportation for manufactured goods that we use every day. It even provides us with life saving medicine. But for all that it provides it is still a mystery. Just two percent of the ocean has been explored.

O is also for oceanographer, a scientist who studies the physical, chemical, geological, and biological aspects of the oceans.

June 8th is Ocean Day! On this day we celebrate the life-giving capacity of our oceans.

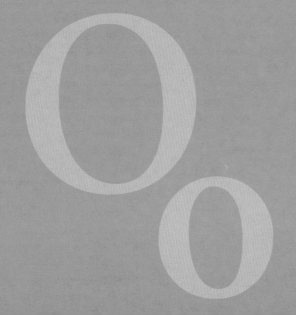

O is for the Oceans.
From an outer space view
our planet Earth is covered
with the color blue.

P is for Penguins—
birds that never fly.
They depend on the ocean
for their food supply.

Pp

Penguins are seabirds; a seabird is a bird that makes its living from the ocean. Penguins live in Antarctica, New Zealand, Australia, Africa, and on the western coast of South America. They are unable to fly in the air but they seem to fly effortlessly through the water in search of food. They eat krill, squid, crabs, and a variety of small fish. Emperor penguins live in the Antarctic and are about 44 inches tall making them the largest of the 17 different kinds of penguins. New Zealand is home to the smallest species of penguin that are about 16 inches tall called the little blue or fairy penguin.

The albatross is a seabird that does fly through the air. Albatrosses use the ocean winds to glide for hours just above the surface. The wandering albatross has the largest wingspan of any bird—up to 11 feet.

P is also for Pressure. Water has weight to it. Salt water is a little heavier than freshwater. The deeper you are in the ocean, the more water that is on top of you, so the more pressure you feel due to the weight of the water. A 10-inch-tall Styrofoam cup sent down in the ocean to a depth of 2,000 meters will come back only one inch tall.

For centuries, royalty and the church controlled the oceans and its waterways. Wars were fought over who had ownership of newly discovered land. It was forbidden by law to share maps and information about the oceans that would help other countries.

Christopher Columbus had to ask King Ferdinand and Queen Isabella of Spain three times before finally getting their permission to go on his voyage of discovery in 1492. They provided him with three ships: the *Nina*, *Pinta*, and *Santa Maria*, 90 crewman, and supplies for his voyage. When he successfully returned to Spain he brought with him natives of the new lands to be used as slaves. Queen Isabella ordered them to be returned to their homes. In her final will she wrote her desire that the "Indians" be treated with justice and fairness. Queen Isabella was the first woman and only foreign ruler to be featured on a United States coin and was the first woman to be featured on a United States postal stamp. The stamp and commemorative coin were produced to celebrate the 400th anniversary of Christopher Columbus's voyage to the new world.

Q is for Queen Isabella.
She gave her permission
for Christopher Columbus to sail
on a special mission.

R r

Ray fish look like birds flapping their wings underwater. They are a flat shaped fish closely related to sharks. Like sharks their bodies are made primarily of cartilage. The smallest ray, the short nose electric ray, is about four inches long and the manta rays are the biggest—they are over 20 feet wide. Ray fish eat mainly plankton, mollusks, crustaceans, worms, and smaller fish. They are not known to attack humans, but they will defend themselves if disturbed. Some rays have deadly barbs or stingers like the stingray. Electric rays or torpedo rays produce electricity to help defend themselves, or to stun their prey before eating them.

R is also for reptiles. Snakes, turtles, and lizards are reptiles that live in the ocean. Seven species of turtles make the ocean their home. The leatherback is the largest sea turtle. It can be more than six feet long and weigh almost 2,000 pounds. The Indo-pacific or saltwater crocodile lives in or near the ocean. The marine iguana is the only ocean dwelling lizard. It lives on the Galapagos Islands and swims into the water for its vegetarian meal of seaweed.

R is for Rays.
Don't shout in alarm.
These strange looking fish
mean you no harm.

Sharks are found in every ocean. There are hundreds of species of sharks. The great white shark is the best-known shark and the most feared. It is the largest predatory fish with huge blade-like teeth. Great whites are between 10 and 21 feet long. Since sharks have a backbone and gills they are a fish but a special kind called *Elasmobranch*. Its skull, backbone, and fins are made out of cartilage. This is the same material that gives your nose and ears their flexibility. Sharks have several rows of teeth. When they lose a tooth another one slides forward to take its place. Some sharks lay eggs, others give birth to their babies called pups. Babies are immediately on their own and fully capable of finding food and caring for themselves. The largest shark is called the whale shark. It can grow more than 50 feet long. They have small teeth that trap tiny fish and crustaceans.

S is also for the Sargasso Sea. In the Atlantic Ocean, there is a large circular current, known as the North Atlantic Gyre. Because some ships and planes have been lost in this area, many people call this area The Bermuda Triangle.

S is for Sharks.
One called the great white is known for its sharp teeth and its incredible bite.

T is for Tides—
    high or low.
The moon and sun
    make them come and go.

T t

Tides are the alternating rise and fall in the oceans' water level caused by the pull of gravity among the Earth, moon, and sun. Tides usually change the water level 3 to 9 feet but the water level in the Bay of Fundy between New Brunswick and Nova Scotia changes as much as 57 feet between tides. When tides go out they leave behind water trapped on rocky shores called tide pools. These can be small or large pools of water. Sea creatures and plants found in these pools have adapted to live in a constantly changing environment.

T is also for *tsunami* (soo-NAH-mee), a series of ocean waves that form under-water as a result of the sudden movement in the ocean floor caused by an earth-quake or volcanic eruption. The tsunami wave may come gently ashore with just a bump or it may grow to be a fast moving wall of unstoppable water. A tsunami can cause terrible damage and destruction. An earthquake in the Indian Ocean caused one of the largest and most recent tsunami waves on December 26, 2004 referred to as the Asian Tsunami.

The narwhal, also known as the unicorn of the sea, is actually a whale with a spiral-shaped tooth that can grow up to ten feet in length. Narwhals spend their time in Arctic waters and never migrate like other whales. Long before TV, radio, or the Internet, people hadn't heard anything about narwhal whales with their unusual twisted tooth. Traveling traders and sailors took advantage of this lack of knowledge and claimed the narwhal's tooth was from a unicorn. Whales are divided into two groups—toothed whales and baleen whales. Toothed whales have teeth and hunt for food such as fish and squid. Baleen whales have fibrous material called baleen that they use to strain tiny shrimp called krill and fish by gulping large amounts of water into their huge mouths.

When water from deep beneath the ocean moves up towards the surface it is called upwelling—another **U** word. This happens when the wind blows ocean water toward the eastern shores of the ocean piling up the water into a mound. To replace the water pushed away from the western coast-line, cooler water flows up from the ocean depths bringing nutrients for oceanic plants and animals to grow.

U u

U is for the Unicorn.
These creatures still exist.
The narwhal of the arctic
has a long tooth with a twist!

V is for Volcanoes
on the ocean floor.
Sometimes they make islands
where nothing was before.

A volcano is a place where magma seeps out from the Earth's interior. Islands made out of volcanoes first start on the ocean floor. Volcanic islands are taller from the ocean floor to sea level than they are from sea level to their highest peak. Some of these volcanic islands that were once under the ocean are: Hawaii, Japan, the Azores, and the Marianas. Lo'ihi is the youngest Hawaiian volcano but has not yet gotten past sea level. A circle of volcanoes called the "ring of fire" located in the Pacific Ocean is believed to have 500 active volcanoes that haven't reached the surface of the ocean. Indonesia has 70 volcanoes—the most in one country.

V is also for vents. Hypothermal vents are holes in the ocean floor that let out boiling water from deep within the Earth. Giant clams, mussels, and red frilled tubeworms about 10 feet long thrive in this unique ocean environment.

The wind creates waves. Wave size depends on the wind strength, duration and the distance it travels over the water. The crest is the top of the wave. The trough is the bottom of a wave. The distance between the two gives you the height of a wave. The distance between two crests gives you the wave width.

A surfer is someone who takes advantage of waves. Using surfboards they ride to shore on the crest of a wave. Duke Kahanamoku born August 24, 1890 in Honolulu, Hawaii is considered the father of modern day surfing. He grew up on the beaches of Hawaii mastering the ancient Hawaiian tradition of surfing. After becoming an Olympic gold medal winner he traveled to beaches around the world giving demonstrations of surfing.

W is also for weather. The ocean's ability to store heat during the day then release it at night helps keep the temperature of the Earth stable. The ocean is where tropical cyclones start. Tropical cyclones have winds of 74 miles per hour or higher. Depending on what part of the oceans you are talking about these storms can be called hurricanes or typhoons.

W
W

W is for Waves.
   Surfers look for the best
   to ride their boards
      on top of the crest.

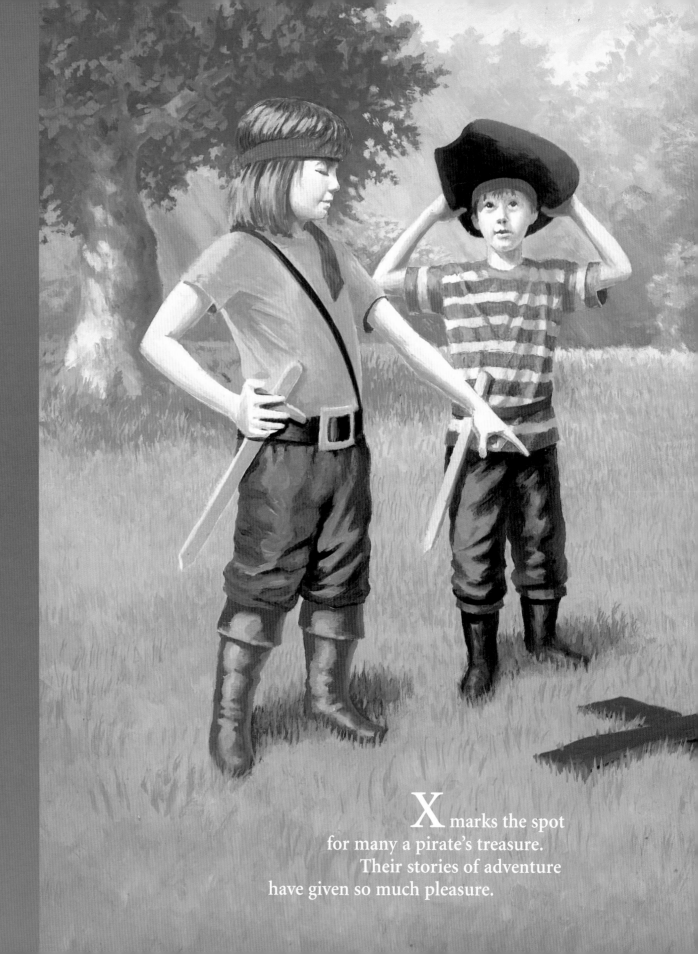

You might have heard tales of the Pirate Blackbeard and his evil ways. His real name was Edward Teach. Legend says that Blackbeard died before he told anyone where he buried all of his treasure. Many people have searched for his chests of gold and jewels but no one has ever found them. Another pirate was Bartholomew Roberts, known as "Black Bart." He never drank anything stronger than tea, never worked on the Sabbath, and always went to bed early! He was considered the most successful pirate that ever lived. Women were also pirates. Anne Bonny and Mary Read were two women who dressed like men and became pirates.

A privateer was a pirate with permission from a government to seize or destroy a merchant vessel of another nation. This permission caused a huge increase in the number of pirates and plundering of ships. Countries finally wanted to stop all the plundering, so in 1856 they got together to sign an agreement called the Declaration of Paris that would outlaw any privateering. But some important countries during that time—Mexico, Spain, and the United States—refused to sign the declaration.

X

X

X marks the spot
for many a pirate's treasure.
Their stories of adventure
have given so much pleasure.

Y is for Yellow-bellied sea snake.
They have a distinctive tail.
It's shaped like a paddle
with bright and colorful detail.

Yy

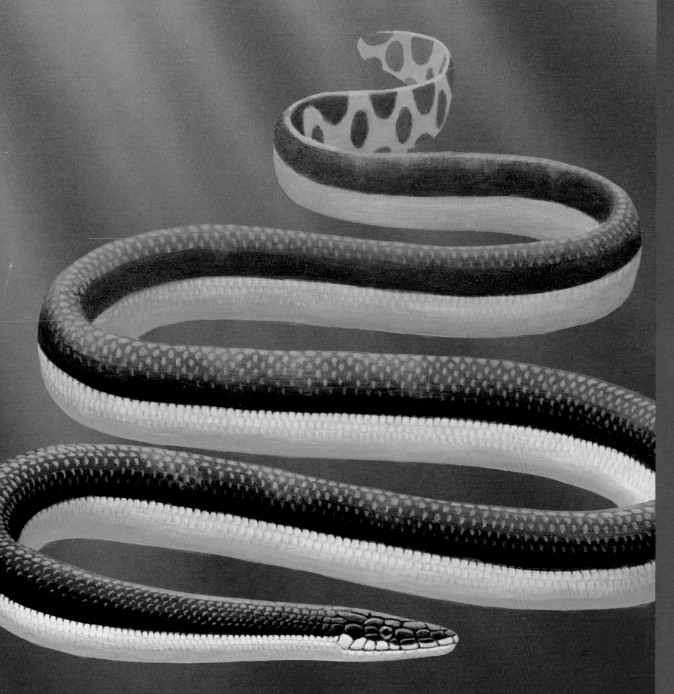

Sea snakes are reptiles; they have a backbone, breathe air, and their body temperature changes with the temperature of their environment. Their flat and paddle-shaped tail helps them travel through water. The nostrils on top of their heads make it easy for them to breath air while swimming on top of the water. When they dive their nostrils close. Yellow-bellied snakes are venomous snakes. They use their venom to paralyze prey—mainly fish and eels. Yellow-bellied snakes usually have four babies which are about 12 inches long. The mothers give birth in areas with enough food to help the babies get started but once they are born, the babies are on their own. Yellow-bellied snakes are *pelagic* (puh-LAJ-ik) sea snakes. That means they never leave the ocean.

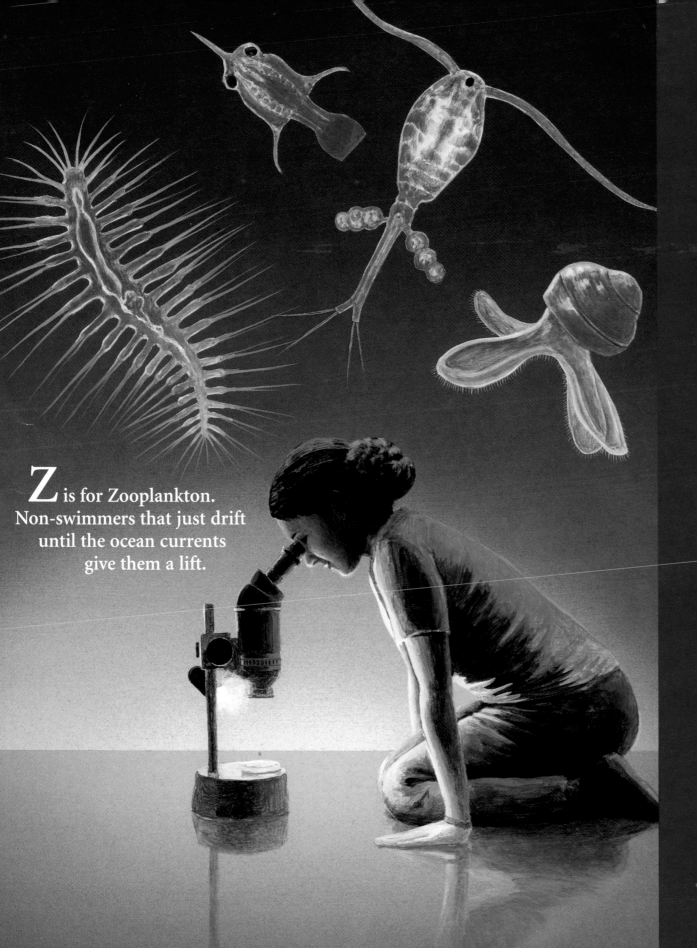

Plankton are tiny sea animals and plants that drift in the ocean's currents and waves. Plankton is the foundation of the ocean food chain. *Zooplankton* (ZOH-uh-plank-tun), tiny sea animals, are eaten by fish, birds, and mammals. Zooplankton eat other plankton including phytoplankton. *Phytoplankton* (FIE-tuh-plank-tun) are tiny plants that use energy from the sun and available chemicals such as carbon dioxide to make into food for themselves and others. This process is called photosynthesis. It produces oxygen as a byproduct. Of all the sea creatures and plants that we have talked about in the ocean the very smallest are the most important to our existence and we depend on them for the very air that we breathe.

Another **Z** word is *zooxanthellae* (zoo-eh-THE-lee): single-celled plants that live inside the polyps that build coral. They have a *symbiotic* (sim-bee-OH-tic) relationship with polyps—that means they help each other. The polyps provide wastes that the plants use as food. The plants provide oxygen and food for the polyps. The plants give the polyp color. When zooanthellae die or leave the coral colony the colony turns white. When this happens it is referred to as coral bleaching. It is a sign that something has gone wrong with the symbiotic relationship between the coral polyps and the zooanthellae.

Z is for Zooplankton.
Non-swimmers that just drift
until the ocean currents
give them a lift.

Zz

Marie and Roland Smith

Marie and Roland grew up in Oregon and live on a small farm south of Portland. Roland is the author of many award-winning books for children including *Peak*, *Thunder Cave*, *Sasquatch*, *Jaguar*, *Zach's Lie*, and *The Captain's Dog: My Journey with the Lewis and Clark Tribe*, which won the Pacific Northwest Bookseller's Award. *W is for Waves* is the fifth book Marie and Roland have written together.

John Megahan

John studied both science and art and in the early 90s decided to combine his interests in art and biology and became a biological illustrator. He is currently a Senior Biological Illustrator at the University of Michigan's Museum of Zoology and has taught several classes as an adjunct lecturer at the University of Michigan's School of Art. His past work has taken him to work on salmon in eastern Oregon, salamanders in western Oregon, marbled murrelets and sea lions on the Oregon coast, and marine invertebrates in Oregon and Alaska. John has also done freelance work for Weyerhaeuser Company, St. Martin's Press, MIT press, The American Fisheries Society, Arizona Highways, Oregon State University, and others. John and his family live in Ann Arbor, Michigan.